Twenty to

Tatted Snowflakes

Jennifer Williams

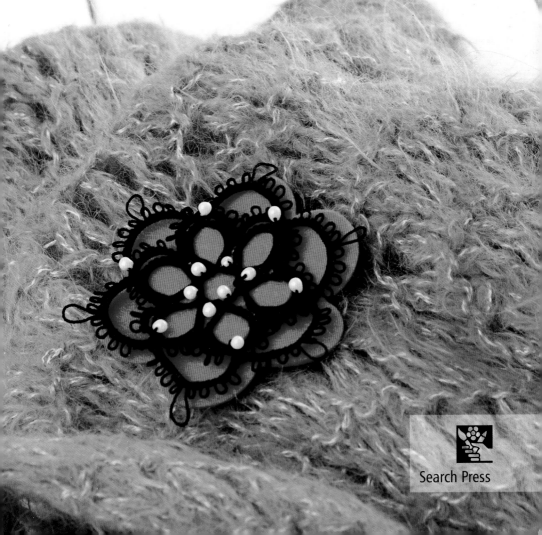

Search Press

First published in 2015

Search Press Limited
Wellwood, North Farm Road,
Tunbridge Wells, Kent TN2 3DR

Text and diagram copyright © Jennifer Williams
2015

Photographs by Neal Grundy at
Search Press Studios

Photographs and design copyright
© Search Press Ltd 2015

Print ISBN: 978-1-78221-227-0
ebook ISBN: 978-1-78126-270-2

The Publishers and author can accept no
responsibility for any consequences arising from
the information, advice or instructions given in
this publication.

Readers are permitted to reproduce any of the
items in this book for their personal use, or for
the purposes of selling for charity, free of charge
and without the prior permission of the Publishers.
Any use of the items for commercial purposes is
not permitted without the prior permission of
the Publishers.

Suppliers
If you have difficulty in obtaining any of the
materials and equipment mentioned in this book,
then please visit the Search Press website for
details of suppliers: www.searchpress.com

Printed in China

Dedication
To my children for their
encouragement and support.

Abbreviations

ds	double stitch. This is usually omitted and the pattern has just the number of double stitches to be worked
R.	ring
CH.	chain
p	picot – open measurement 5mm (¼in); use an opened-out paperclip as a picot gauge
vsp	very small picot; just big enough to insert a size 0.75mm (US 13) crochet hook
mp	medium picot – 7mm (¼in) open measurement; use a cocktail stick as a picot gauge
Lp	large picot – 1cm (½in) open measurement; use a coffee stirrer or short double-ended 3.25mm (US 3) knitting needle
vbp	very big picot – 2cm (¾in) open measurement; use a pencil or similar as a picot gauge
dpb	dropped picot to the back – 3 second half stitches, picot or bead, 3 first half stitches
dpf	dropped picot to the front – 3 first half stitches, picot or bead, 3 second half stitches
Beaded dpb or beaded dpf	dropped picot with 1 or 3 beads in place of the 'picot'
cl	close ring
RW	reverse work
+	join
sj	shuttle join
B	bead, so 3B = three beads
SH.1	shuttle 1
DNRW	do not reverse work
CTM	continuous thread method
SS	swap shuttles
LC	lock chain (turn the first half of the double stitch as usual, but do not turn the second half of the double stitch)
sms	small sequin
JR.	Josephine ring (a double stitch followed by a number, usually 12, second half stitches)
SLT	Shoelace Trick (make an overhand tie so that the threads change place)
Tension	to push the double stitches close together, or spread them out, in order to make a chain curve

Contents

Introduction

Snowflakes are usually associated with winter and we copy their delicate shapes to make tree decorations and embellishments to go on Christmas cards. However, the snowflake shape is too pretty to be confined to just this time of year and they look beautiful worked in colours, with coloured beads or sequins.

Tatted snowflakes can be used in many different ways: to hang in windows, on Christmas trees or to decorate a greetings card, for example. I have used the designs in this book to embellish some gloves, a tea light holder and a scarf – and I have made one of them into a pendant and earrings set. The patterns are suitable for tatters with just the basic tatting skills because explanations for any other techniques are incorporated in the instructions. Other useful techniques can be found on pages 6 and 7.

Most of the designs are tatted without the addition of any embellishments, but I have added beads to others to give them a different dimension – and a bit of 'bling'. The beads used are mostly round seed or 4mm ($^3/_{16}$in) beads but I have also used drop beads, which are pear-shaped. The designs named Anne and Karen have large sequins, which are known as 'spangles', enclosed between two tatted circles at their centres, and Karen has small sequins on the tatted chains as well.

Arwenna and Hannah incorporate small buttons and Lynn and Eileen have been tatted onto small plastic curtain rings.

I really enjoyed designing these snowflakes and I hope you will have fun tatting them.

Tools and techniques

Tatting is a very portable craft requiring as little equipment as a shuttle, small crochet hook, scissors, thread and a pattern. You can include another shuttle or two, beads, needles to string the beads and to sew in the ends on your finished piece of tatting, a second, very fine crochet hook and jewellery findings.

Threads   The designs in this book have been tatted using size 20 or 10 crochet cotton, but you can tat with any thickness of thread provided it is smooth. For best results, use the thread that is stipulated by the designer.

Shuttles   These can be made from wood, metal, bone and horn, but are usually plastic. Some have a removable spool in the centre to hold the thread, while others have a 'post' in the centre, round which to wind the thread. Shuttles are pointed at both ends, so look boat-shaped, or they can have a metal hook added

to one end. Other shuttles have an extension at one end forming a 'pick' which is used, like the hook, to make joins between two elements of tatting.

Crochet hook   A small size 0.75mm (US 13) steel hook is used to draw a loop through a picot on another element of your tatting so that you can make a join. A fine hook (size 0.4mm/US 16) is used to add beads to picots, before working a join, and also to add just a few beads to the thread.

Needles   Big Eyed Needles are split from end to end, so are very useful when stringing beads on any thickness of thread. Beading needles are used in conjunction with a fine sewing thread for stringing beads. Size 18 or 16 tapestry needles are used for sewing in loose ends of thread, to hide them, when you have finished your piece of tatting.

Shuttle join

This type of join is used when the working shuttle thread is nearer to the picot, or small space, to which the join is to be made, than the auxiliary (ball) thread.

1 Draw a loop in the shuttle thread up through the picot, or small space, indicated in the pattern.

2 Pass the shuttle through this loop, then adjust the threads to bring the previous stitches close to the join.

3 Pull the shuttle to close the join.

Folded join

The folded join is a technique that helps you to join the last ring to the first ring in a design.

1 Work the final ring as far as the join.

2 Fold the motif away from you, bringing the first ring in place behind your work and matching it up with the final ring.

3 Insert a crochet hook through the picot that you wish to join to **from the back**.

4 Hook the working thread (the one round your hand, not the shuttle thread) and draw a loop through the joining picot.

5 Now pass the shuttle through the loop from front to back. Make sure the loop has not twisted.

6 Adjust the threads as for a normal join, then work a second half stitch.

7 Complete the ring according to the pattern.

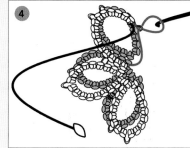

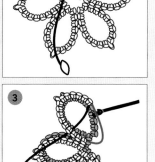
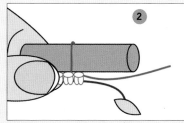

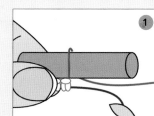
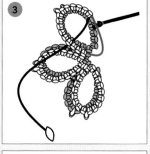

Picot gauge

Where used in this book, the picot gauge is held parallel to the core thread.

1 The thread from your hand goes up and over to the back of the picot gauge.

2 Work the following stitch next to the double stitch before the picot.

Alison

Materials:

Size 20 thread

Tools:

2 x shuttles

1 x crochet hook, size 0.75mm (US 13)

Small pair of scissors

Instructions:

Wind two shuttles CTM with 5m (5½yd) of thread onto shuttle 1 and 2.5m (2¾yd) onto shuttle 2.

SH.1 R.A 8, p, 6, p, 2, cl

R.B 2, + to previous ring, 6, mp, 2, Lp, 2, mp, 6, p, 2, cl

R.C 2, + to previous ring, 6, p, 8, cl, RW

CH. 6, SS, DNRW

SH.2 R.D 4, p, 4, p, 4, cl, SS, DNRW

SH.1 CH. 6, RW

SH 1

(UP FACE)

    *R.E 8, + to last ring on previous three-ring group, 6, p, 2, cl

R.F 2, + to previous ring, 6, mp, 2, Lp, 2, mp, 6, p, 2, cl

R.G 2, + to previous ring, 6, p, 8, cl, RW

CH. 6, SS, DNRW

SH.2 R.H 4, + to previous ring off chain, 4, p, 4, cl, SS, DNRW

SH.1 CH. 6, RW**

Repeat from * to ** four times, remembering to join ring W to ring A and ring X to ring D on the last repeat (see diagram).

Cut and tie to the base of rings A, B and C. Secure all the ends. Block and stiffen as required.

SS = SWAP SHUTTLES

Auriel

Materials:

Size 20 thread

Tools:

1 x shuttle

1 x crochet hook, size 0.75mm (US 13)

Small pair of scissors

3 x picot gauges graded in size – for example, an opened paper clip for 'p', a cocktail stick for 'mp' and a short size 3¼mm double-ended knitting needle for 'Lp'

Instructions:

Row 1 (see diagram 1)

Wind about 2.5m (2¾yd) onto the shuttle. Do not cut.

R.A	6, p, 3, p, 6, cl
R.B	6, p, 3, p, 6, cl, RW
CH.	5, p, 5, RW
*R.C	6, + to previous ring, 3, p, 6, cl
R.D	6, p, 3, p, 6, cl, RW
CH.	5, p, 5 **

Repeat from * to ** three more times then

R.K	6, + to previous ring, 3, p, 6, cl
R.L	6, p, 3, + to ring A, 6, cl, RW
CH.	5, p, 5

Cut and tie to the base of rings A and B then secure the ends.

Row 2 (see diagrams 2 and 3)

Wind about 4m (4½yd) of thread onto the shuttle. Do not cut.

R.A	6, p, 3, + to the left-hand ring of one of the two ring groups on row 1, 6, cl
R.B	6, + to the right hand ring of the same two ring group on row 1, 3, p, 6, cl, RW
CH.	10, tension, RW
R.C	6, + to ring B, 3, p, 6, cl, RW
CH.	3, p, 2, mp, 2, Lp, 2, mp, 2, p, 3, tension, RW
R.D	6, + to ring C, 3, p, 6, cl, RW
CH.	10, tension, RW
*R.E	6, + to previous ring, 3, + to the adjacent ring on row 1, 6, cl
R.F	6, + to the adjacent ring on row 1, 3, p, 6, cl, RW
CH.	10, tension, RW
R.G	6, + to previous ring, 3, p, 6, cl, RW
CH.	3, p, 2, mp, 2, LP, 2, mp, 2, p, 3, tension, RW#
R.H	6, + to previous ring, 3, p, 6, cl, RW
CH.	10, tension, RW**

Repeat from * to ** three more times then repeat from * to # and continue:

R.X	6, + to ring W, 3, + to ring A, 6, cl, RW
CH.	10, tension

Cut and tie to the base of rings A and B then secure the ends. Block and stiffen as required.

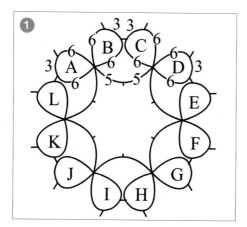

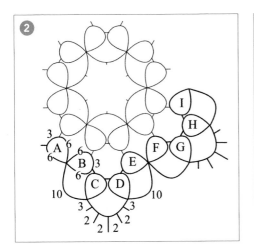

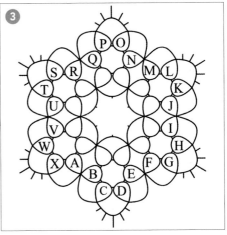

Helen

Materials:

Size 20 thread

66 x size 11 beads

Tools:

1 x shuttle

1 x crochet hook, size 0.4mm (US 16)

Small pair of scissors

Instructions:

Row 1 (see diagram 1)

String 6 of the beads then wind about 1.5m (1¾yd) of thread onto the shuttle, leaving the beads on the ball thread.

R.A   4, p, 4, p, 4, p, 4, cl, RW

CH.   2, B, 2, RW

*R.B   4, p, 4, p, 4, p, 4, cl, RW

CH.   2, B, 2, RW**

Repeat from * to ** four more times.

Cut and tie to the base of ring A then secure the ends.

Row 2

String 54 beads then wind about 4.5m (5yd) of thread onto the shuttle along with the beads.

R.G   Bring 1 bead (from the shuttle) into the ring round your hand:

       8, B, 5, p, 3, cl (see diagram 2)

R.H   Bring 7 beads (from the shuttle) into the ring round your hand:

       3, + to ring G, 3, B, 2, B, 2, 3B, 2, B, 2, B, 3, p, 3, cl

R.I   Bring 1 bead (from the shuttle) into the ring round your hand:

       3, + to ring H, 5, B, 8, cl, RW

LC.   8, add a bead (using the fine crochet hook) to the middle picot on one of the rings on row 1, 8, RW

*R.J   Bring 1 bead (from the shuttle) into the ring round your hand:

       8, B, 5, p, 3, cl (see diagram 3)

R.K   Bring 7 beads (from the shuttle) into the ring round your hand:

       3, + to previous ring, 3, B, 2, B, 2, 3B, 2, B, 2, B, 3, p, 3, cl

R.L   Bring 1 bead (from the shuttle) into the ring round your hand:

       3, + to previous ring, 5, B, 8, cl, RW

LC.   8, add a bead (using the fine crochet hook) to the middle picot on the adjacent ring on row 1, 8, RW**

Repeat from * to ** four more times (see diagram 4) then cut and tie to the base of rings G, H and I. Secure the ends.

Block and stiffen as required.

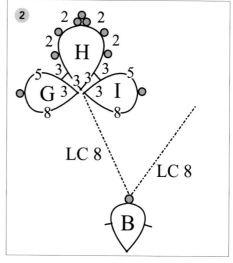

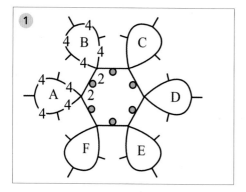

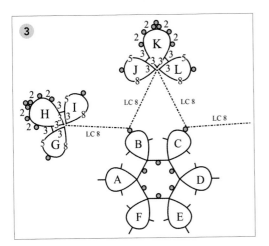

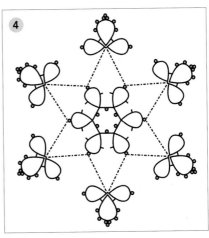

Gillian

Materials:

Size 20 thread

42 x size 11 beads

Instructions:

String 42 beads then wind about 1.5m (1¾yd) of thread onto the shuttle along with 6 of the beads. Do not cut.

Row 1

R.A   Bring 6 beads into the ring round your hand:

      6, 6B, 6, cl, RW

CH.   6, 3B, 6, RW (see diagram 1)

*R.B   6, move one of the beads on ring A to the left then + to the picot, 6, cl, RW

CH.   6, 3B, 6, cl, RW** (see diagram 2)

Tools:

1 x shuttle

1 x crochet hook, size 0.75mm (US 13)

Small pair of scissors

Repeat from * to ** four more times but do not reverse work after the fourth repeat.

Work a sj into the base of ring A (see diagram 3). Do not cut.

Row 2

CH.   8, 3B, 8, sj into the base of the adjacent ring

Repeat this chain five more times, omitting the final shuttle join, then cut and tie to the base of ring A (see diagram 4).

Block and stiffen as required.

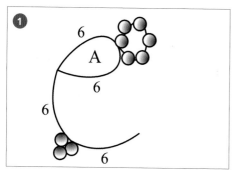

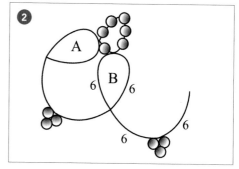

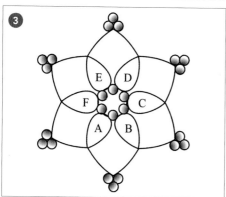

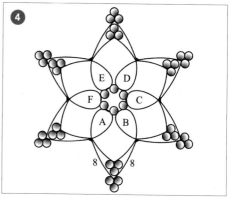

Catrin

Materials:

Size 20 thread

Tools:

1 x shuttle

1 x crochet hook, 0.75mm (US 13)

Small pair of scissors

Tapestry needle

Instructions:

Row 1

Wind about 1.5m (1¾yd) of thread onto the shuttle. Do not cut (see diagram 1).

R.A   2, (p, 2) x 5, cl, RW

CH.   18, tension to measure 2cm (¾in), RW

*R.B   2, p, 2, + to the 4th picot on the previous ring, 2, (p, 2) x 3, cl, RW

CH.   18, tension to measure 2cm (¾in), RW**

Repeat from * to ** three times more then

R.F   2, p, 2, + to the second free picot on ring E, 2, p, 2, join to the middle free picot on ring A, 2, p, 2, cl, RW

CH.   18, tension to measure 2cm (¾in)

Cut and tie to the base of ring A then secure the ends.

Row 2

Wind about 3.5m (3¾yd) of thread onto the shuttle. Do not cut.

*R.G   6, p, 4, p, 2, cl

R.H   2, + to previous ring, 4, (p, 2) x 4, p, 4, p, 2, cl (see diagram 2)

R.I   2, + to previous ring, 4, p, 6, cl, RW

CH.   22, tension to measure 2cm (¾in), RW**

Repeat from * to ** five more times.

Cut and tie to the base of rings G, H and I, then secure the ends (see diagram 3).

Assembling the snowflake

Place row 1 inside row 2 (see diagam 4), then draw each of the three ring groups, in turn, through the chains on row 1 (see diagram 5). Block and stiffen as required.

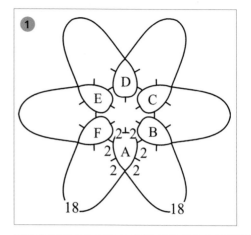

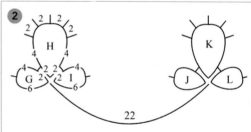

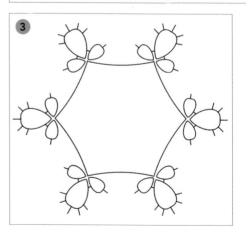

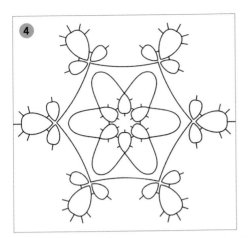

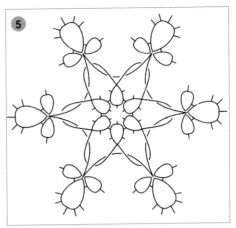

Karen

Materials:

Size 20 thread

1 x 2cm (¾in) sequin or disc

48 x small sequins

Tools:

1 x shuttle

2 x crochet hooks, size 0.75mm and 0.4mm (US 13 and 16)

1 x Big Eyed Needle or beading needle

Small pair of scissors

Instructions:

Row 1 (see diagram 1)

Wind about 1.25m (1½yd) of thread onto the shuttle. Do not cut.

R.A   6, p, 2, p, 6, cl, RW

CH.   4, + sms, 4, RW

R.B   6, + (to 2nd 'p' on previous ring), 2, p, 6, cl, RW

CH.   4, + sms, 4, RW

*RC   6, + (to 'p' on previous ring), 2, p, 6, cl, RW

CH.   4, + sms, 4, RW

Repeat from * twice more (5 rings and chains).

R.F   6, + (to 'p' on previous ring), 2, + (to picot on ring A), 6, cl, RW

CH.   4, + sms, 4,

Cut and tie to the base of ring A.

Row 2 (see diagram 2)

Wind about 1.25m (1½yd) of thread onto the shuttle. Do not cut.

R.A   6, p, 2, p, 6, cl, RW

CH.   6, + sms, 4, sms, 6, RW

R.B   6, + (to 2nd 'p' on previous ring), 2, p, 6, cl, RW

CH.   6, + sms, 4, sms, 6, RW

*RC   6, + (to 'p' on previous ring), 2, p, 6, cl, RW

CH.   6, + sms, 4, sms, 6, RW

Repeat from * twice more (5 rings and chains).

R.F   6, + (to 'p' on previous ring), 2, + (to picot on ring A), 6, cl, RW

CH.   6, + sms, 4, sms, 6

Cut and tie to the base of ring A.

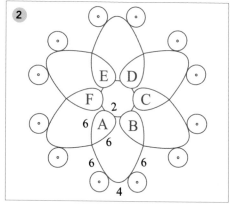

Row 3 (see diagrams 3 and 4)

Wind about 2m (2¼yd) of thread onto the shuttle. Do not cut.

Place row 1 on top of row 2, lining up the rings.

R.A   8, + to the base of ring A on row 1 and the base of ring A on row 2 together, 8, cl, RW

CH.   5, (+ sms, 4) x 4, sms, 5, RW

*R.B   8, + to the base of the adjacent ring on row 1 and the base of the adjacent ring on row 2 together, 8, cl, RW

CH.   5, (+ sms, 4) x 4, sms, 5, RW**

Repeat from * to ** to the end of row, remembering to slip the large sequin in between rows 1 and 2 before joining the fifth ring. Cut and tie to the base of ring A.

Block and stiffen as required.

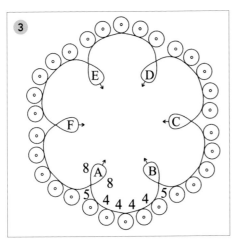

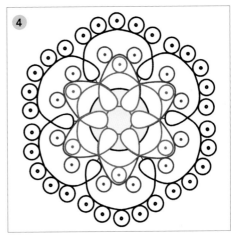

Mary

Materials:

Size 20 thread

66 x size 11 beads

Tools:

1 x shuttle

1 x crochet hook, size
0.4mm (US 16)

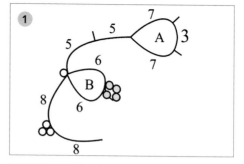

Instructions:

String 54 of the beads and wind about 3.5m (3¾yd) of thread onto the shuttle with 24 beads, leaving 30 beads on the ball thread. The remaining 12 beads are added to picots before working joins, using the fine crochet hook.

R.A   (See diagram 1) 7, p, 3, p, 7, cl, RW

CH.   5, p, 5, RW

R.B   Bring 4 beads into the ring round your hand
      6, 4B, 6, cl, RW

CH.   Move one bead up on the ball thread
      8, 3B, 8, RW

R.C   (See diagram 2) 6, + to the beaded picot on ring 'B' with 1 bead to the left of the join and 3 beads to the right of the join, 6, cl, RW

CH.   Move up a bead on the ball thread
      5, p, 5, RW

R.D   7, add a bead to the second picot on ring A using the crochet hook, 3, p, 7, cl, RW

*CH.   (See diagram 3) 5, add a bead and join to the picot on the previous chain, 5, RW

R.E   Bring 4 beads into the ring round your hand
      6, 4B, 6, cl, RW (see diagram 3)

CH.   Move up a bead on the ball thread
      8, 3B, 8, RW

R.F   6, + to the beaded picot on the previous ring with 1 bead to the left of the join and 3 beads to the right of the join, 6, cl, RW

CH.   Move up a bead on the ball thread
      5, p, 5, RW***

R.G   7, add a bead and join to the free picot on the adjacent centre ring, 3, p, 7, cl, RW**

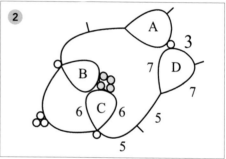

Repeat from * to ** twice more, then from * to *** once more.

R.P   (See diagram 4) 7, add a bead and join to the free picot on the adjacent centre ring, 3, add a bead and join to the free picot on ring A, 7, cl, RW

CH.   5, add a bead and join to the picot on the previous chain, 5, RW

R.Q   Bring 4 beads into the ring round your hand
      6, 4B, 6, cl, RW

CH.   Move up a bead on the ball thread
      8, 3B, 8, RW

R.R   6, + to the beaded picot on the previous ring with 1 bead to the left of the join and 3 beads to the right of the join, 6, cl, RW

CH.   Move up a bead on the ball thread 5, add a bead and join to the first chain, 5

Cut and tie to the base of ring A. Secure the ends. Block and stiffen as required.

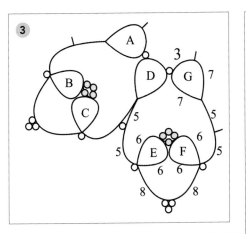

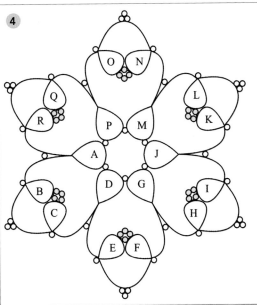

Jan

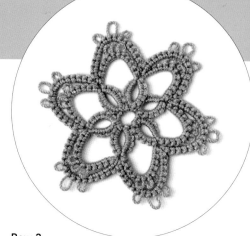

Materials:

Size 20 thread

Tools:

1 x shuttle

1 x crochet hook, size 0.75mm (US 13)

Small pair of scissors

Instructions:

Wind about 1.5m (1¾yd) of thread onto the shuttle. Do not cut.

Row 1

R.A   6, large picot (1 cm), 6, cl, RW

CH.   5, p, 1, p, 1, p, 5, RW (see diagram 1)

*R.B   6, + to picot on ring A, 6, cl, RW

CH.   5, p, 1, p, 1, p, 5, RW** (see diagram 2)

Repeat from * to ** four more times but do not reverse work after the fourth repeat.

Work a shuttle join (sj) into the base of ring A (see diagram 3).

Do not cut.

Row 2

CH.   6, mp, 2, Lp, 2, mp, 6, sj into the base of the adjacent ring.

Repeat this chain five more times, omitting the final shuttle join, then cut and tie to the base of ring A (see diagram 4).

Block and stiffen as required.

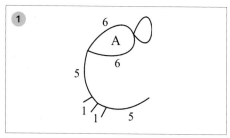

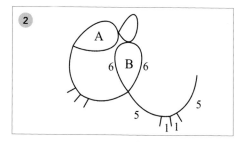

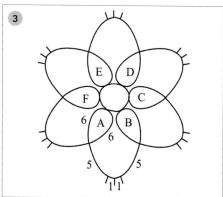

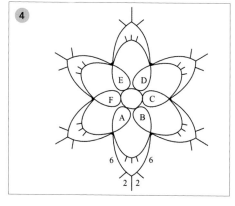

22

Julia

Materials:
Size 20 thread

Tools:
2 x shuttles

1 x crochet hook, size 0.75mm (US 13)

Tapestry needle or beading needle

Small pair of scissors

Special stitch:
Josephine ring: work a double stitch, then 12 second half stitches, close the ring.

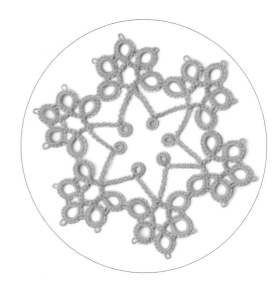

Instructions:
Wind two shuttles CTM with about 7m (7½yd) of thread on shuttle 1 and 2.5m (2¾yd) of thread on shuttle 2 (see diagram 1).

SH.2 JR.A 1, 12 second half stitches, cl, DNRW, SS (see diagram 1)

SH.1 LC. 6

CH. 1, vsp, 2, RW

R.B 8, p, 5, p, 3, cl, RW

CH. 3, RW

R.C 3, + to previous ring, 5, p, 5, p, 3, cl, RW

CH. 3, RW

R.D 3, + to previous ring, 5, p, 5, p, 3, cl, RW

CH. 3, RW

R.E 3, + to previous ring, 5, p, 5, p, 3, cl, RW

CH. 3, RW

R.F 3, + to previous ring, 5, p, 8, cl, RW

CH. 2, + to vsp on the chain before ring B, 1

LC. 6, DNRW, SS (see diagram 2)

*SH.2 JR.G 1, 12 second half stitches, cl, DNRW, SS

SH.1 LC. 6

CH. 1, vsp, 2, RW

R.H 8, + to last ring of the previous group of five rings, 5, p, 3, cl, RW

CH. 3, RW

R.I 3, + to previous ring, 5, p, 5, p, 3, cl, RW

CH. 3, RW

R.J 3, + to previous ring, 5, p, 5, p, 3, cl, RW

CH. 3, RW

R.K 3, + to previous ring, 5, p, 5, p, 3, cl, RW

CH. 3, RW**

R.L 3, + to previous ring, 5, p, 8, cl, RW

CH. 2, + to vsp on the chain before the 1st ring of the five-ring group of rings, 1

LC. 6, DNRW, SS***

Repeat from * to *** three more times, then from * to **.

SH.1 R.Z 3, + to previous ring, 5, + to ring B, 8, cl, RW (see diagram 2)

CH. 2, + to vsp on the chain before the 1st ring of the five-ring group of rings, 1

LC. 6

Cut and tie to the base of JR.A. Block and stiffen as required.

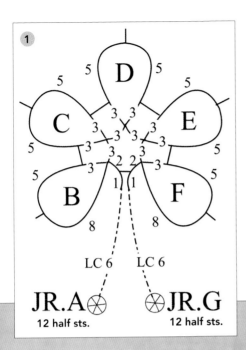

1

5 5
D
5
C 3 3 E
3 3 3 3
5 3 3 3 3 3 5
3 2 2 3
B 1 1 F 5
8 8

LC 6 LC 6

JR.A ⊗ ⊗ JR.G
12 half sts. 12 half sts.

2

D
C E
B F
Z I
A G H J
⊗ ⊗ K
L
⊗ ⊗
⊗ ⊗

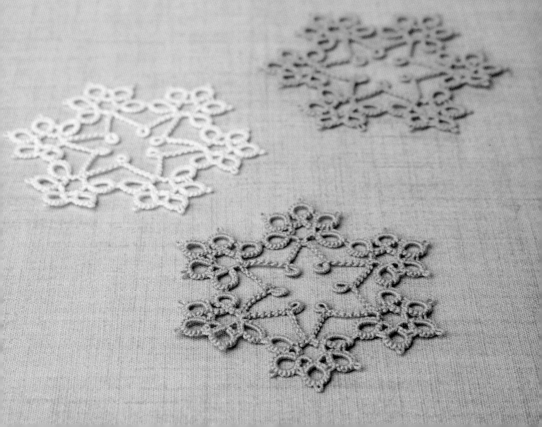

Vivienne

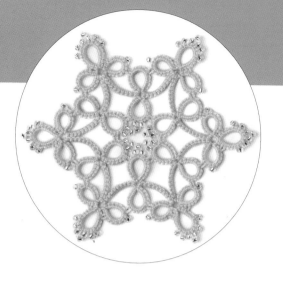

Materials:

Size 20 thread

72 x size 11 beads

Tools:

2 x shuttles

2 x crochet hooks, size 0.75mm and 0.4mm (US 13 and 16)

Tapestry needle or beading needle

Small pair of scissors

Instructions:

String the beads then wind 2 shuttles CTM with 6m (6½yd) of thread and 54 beads onto shuttle 1 and 4m (4½yd) of thread with the remaining 18 beads onto shuttle 2.

Note: the rings shown in red in the diagrams are worked using shuttle 2.

SH.1 R.A (See diagram 1) Bring 1 bead from shuttle 1 into the ring round your hand and work 6, p, 2, B, 6, p, 2, cl

R.B Bring 7 beads into the ring round your hand 2, + to previous ring, 4, B, 2, B, 2, 3B, 2, B, 2, B, 4, p, 2, cl

R.C Bring 1 bead into the ring round your hand 2, + to previous ring, 6, B, 2, p, 6, cl, RW (see diagram 1)

SH.1 CH. 10, RW

R.D 6, + to previous ring, 6, p, 6, cl, RW, SS

SH.2 R.E Bring 3 beads into the ring round your hand and work 6, p, 3, 3B, 3, p, 6, cl, DNRW, SS

SH.1 CH. 10, RW

*R.F (See diagram 2) Bring 1 bead into the ring round your hand 6, + to ring D, 2, B, 6, p, 2, cl

R.G Bring 7 beads into the ring round your hand 2, + to previous ring, 4, B, 2, B, 2, 3B, 2, B, 2, B, 4, p, 2, cl

R.H Bring 1 bead into the ring round your hand 2, + to previous ring, 6, B, 2, p, 6 cl, RW

CH. 10, RW

R.I 6, + to previous ring, 6, p, 6, cl, RW, SS

SH.2 R.J Bring 3 beads into the ring round your hand

6, + to previous centre ring, 3, 3B, 3, p, 6, cl, DNRW, SS

SH.1 CH. 10, RW**

Repeat from * to ** four more times, remembering to join ring Y to rings X and A, and to join centre ring Z to rings U and E (see diagram 3).

Cut and tie to the base of rings A, B and C. Secure the ends. Block and stiffen as required.

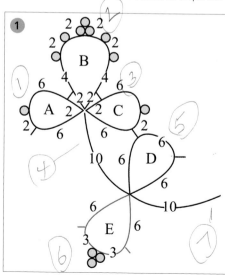

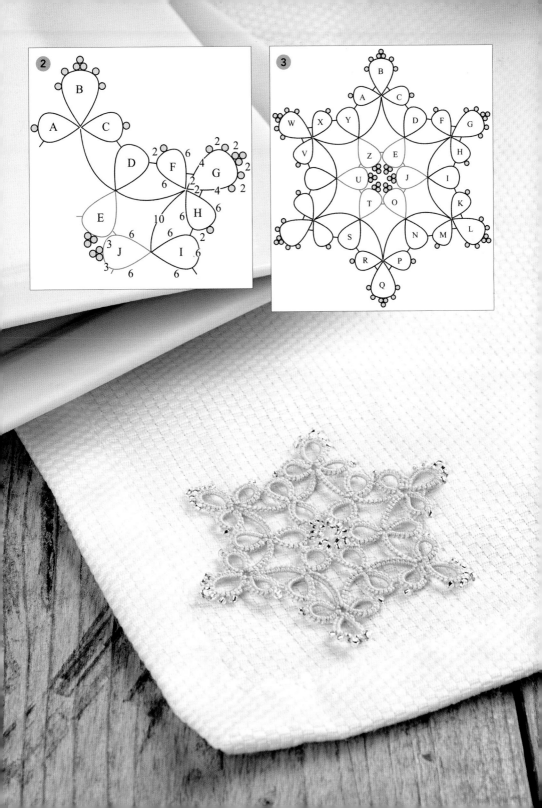

Dinah

Materials:

White and orange size 20 thread

18 x silver and 18 x orange size 11 beads

Tools:

1 x shuttle

1 x crochet hook, size 0.75mm (US 13)

Small pair of scissors

Instructions:

On the white thread string the beads in the following order (silver, orange, silver) x 6 then wind about 2.5m (2¾yd) of thread onto the shuttle, with the beads. Loosely knot the white and orange threads together. The orange thread is the ball thread.

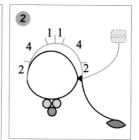

Row 1

*R.   Bring 3 beads into the ring round your hand, 3, 3B, 3, vsp, 10, cl, (see diagram 1), SLT

CH.2, p, 4, p, 1, p, 1, p, 4, p, 2, pull up the chain so that it fits snugly over the outside of the ring above the 10 ds on the ring, sj to the vsp, (see diagram 2) **

Repeat from * to ** five times more (as in diagrams 3 and 4).

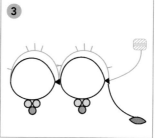

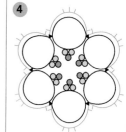

Cut and tie the matching coloured threads to the start of the first ring.

Row 2

On the white thread string the beads in the following order (orange, silver, orange) x 6. Wind about 1m (1yd) of the orange thread onto the shuttle. Knot the white and orange ends together loosely.

Work a shuttle join into the first picot on one of the chains on row 1 and into the last picot on the previous chain (just one shuttle join).

*CH.   1, LC 5, chain 1, move up 3 beads on the white thread, chain 1, LC 5, chain 1, sj to the first picot on the adjacent chain and into the last picot on the previous chain** (see diagram 5).

Repeat from * to ** five times.

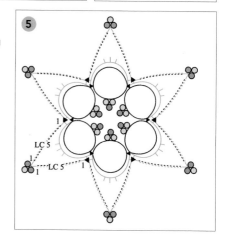

Cut and tie matching coloured threads at the start of the row. Secure all the ends.

Block and stiffen as required.

Lynn

Materials:

Size 20 thread

1 x small curtain ring measuring approximately 15mm (⅝in) in diameter

Tools:

2 x shuttles

1 x crochet hook, size 0.75mm (US 13)

Tapestry needle

Small pair of scissors

Instructions:

Row 1 (see diagrams 1–9)

Wind 2 shuttles CTM with about 2m (2¼yd) of thread onto shuttle 1 and 4.5m (5yd) of thread onto shuttle 2.

Using shuttle 1 (blue in diagrams 1–9), cover the curtain ring with 36 double stitches.

You might find it helpful when you are working row 2 to place a marker, such as a length of contrasting coloured thread, every 6 double stitches. Make an overhand tie with the thread from shuttle 2 at the start of the row. Do not cut.

Row 2 (see diagram 10)

*SH.1 CH. 4, SS, DNRW

SH.2 R.A 6, p, 3, p, 3, cl, SS, DNRW

SH.1 CH. 4, SS, DNRW

SH. 2 R.B 3, + to ring A, 3, p, 2, mp, 2, p, 3, p, 3, cl, SS, DNRW

SH.1 CH. 4, SS, DNRW

SH.2 R.C 3, + to the last picot on ring B, 3, p, 6, cl, SS, DNRW

SH.1 CH. 4, tension the chain to measure about 2cm (¾in) then miss 6 double stitches on row 1 and make a shuttle join between the 6th and 7th double stitch.**

Repeat from * to ** five more times, omitting the shuttle join at the end of the fifth repeat. Cut and tie to the start of the row then secure the ends.

Block and stiffen as required.

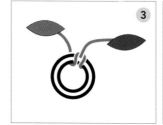

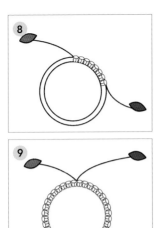

8

9

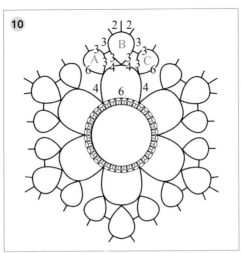

10

Eileen

Materials:

Size 20 thread

1 x small curtain ring measuring approximately 15mm (⁵⁄₈in) in diameter

Tools:

2 x shuttles

3 x picot gauges (an opened-out paper clip for 'p', cocktail stick for 'mp' and pencil for 'vbp')

1 x crochet hook, size 0.75mm (US 13)

Tapestry needle or beading needle

Small pair of scissors

Instructions:

Wind 2 shuttles CTM with about 2m (2¼yd) of thread onto shuttle 1 and 2.5m (2¾yd) of thread onto shuttle 2.

Row 1

Follow the instructions for Lynn on page 30 to cover the curtain ring with 36 double stitches (shuttle 1 = blue in the diagrams). Make an overhand tie with the thread from shuttle 2 at the start of the row. Do not cut. Continue on to the 2nd row.

Row 2 (see diagram 1)

*SH.1	CH.	4, mp, 4, SS, DNRW
SH.2	R.	6, mp, 6, cl, SS, DNRW
SH.1	CH.	4, mp, 4, tension the chain to measure about 2cm (¾in) then count 6 double stitches on row 1 and make a shuttle join between the 6th and 7th double stitch.

Repeat from * five more times omitting the shuttle join at the end of the fifth repeat. Cut and tie to the start of the row then secure ends.

Row 3 (see diagrams 2 and 3)

Wind 2 shuttles CTM with about 4.5m (5yd) of thread onto each shuttle.

SH.1	R.A	6, + to the last picot worked on one of the chains of the 2nd row, 2, + to the first picot worked on the adjacent chain of the 2nd row, 6, cl, RW
	*CH.	8, RW
	R.B	6, + to the 1st ring on the 2nd row, 3, p, 3, cl, RW
	CH.	10, RW
	R.C	4, + to ring B, 2, p, 4, cl, RW, SS
SH.2	R.D	6, p, 2, Lp, 2, p, 6, cl, DNRW, SS
SH.1	CH.	10, RW
	R.E	3, + to ring C, 3, + to the same ring on the 2nd row as ring 'B', 6, cl, RW
	CH.	8, RW***
	R.F	6, + to the last picot on the same chain on the 2nd row, 2, + to the first picot on the adjacent chain, 6, cl, RW**

Repeat from * to ** four more times, then from * to *** once (see diagram 3).

Cut and tie to the base of the start of the row. Block and stiffen as required.

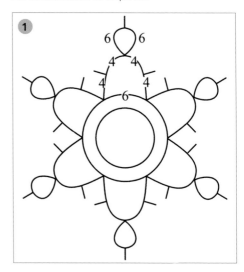

2

6 A 2
6
8

6 B
10 3
4-2 3
C 4 3 E
6 4 3 6
D 10
2 6
2
2 F 6
6
8

3

Arwenna

Materials:

Size 20 thread

6 x 1cm (½in) 4-hole buttons

6 x 3.4mm (⅛in) drop beads

Tools:

1 x shuttle

3 x picot gauges (an opened-out paper clip for 'p',
  cocktail stick for 'mp' and pencil for 'vbp')

2 x crochet hooks, size 0.75mm and 0.4mm (US 13 and 16)

Tapestry needle or beading needle

Small pair of scissors

Instructions:

Row 1

Wind about 1m (1yd) of thread onto the shuttle.
Do not cut.

R.A   (See diagram 1) 6, p, 3, p, 6, cl, RW

CH.   7, + to a button, 7, RW

R.B   6, p, 3, p, 6, cl, RW

CH.   7, + to a different button, 7, RW

R.C   (See diagram 2) 6, + to ring A, 3, p, 6,
       cl, RW

CH.   7, + to a different button, 7, RW

R.D   6, + to ring B, 3, p, 6, cl, RW

CH.   7, + to a different button, 7, RW

R.E   6, + to ring C, 3, + to ring A, 6, cl, RW

CH.   7, + to a different button, 7, RW

R.F   6, + to ring D, 3, + to ring B, 6, cl, RW

CH.   7, + to a different button, 7

Cut and tie to the base of ring A then secure
the ends.

Row 2 (see diagram 3)

String the 6 drop beads then wind about 6m
(6½yd) onto the shuttle, leaving the beads on
the ball thread. Do not cut (see diagram 3).

*R.A   8, + to one of the buttons making the
       join to the hole that is directly opposite
       the one that is joined to row 1, 8, cl, RW

CH.   9, p, 2, RW

R.B   8, + to the hole in the same button that
       is to the right of the previous join, 8, cl

R.C   8, + to the first free hole in the adjacent
       button on row 1, 8, cl, RW

CH.   2, + to the previous chain, 9, RW

R.D   8, + to the same button in the hole that

is directly opposite the one that is
joined to row 1, 8, cl, RW

CH.   9, move up the drop bead, 9, RW**

Repeat from * to ** five times more, then sj
to the base of ring A and continue onto row 3
without cutting the threads.

Row 3 (see diagram 3)

*CH.   2, (mp, 2) x 4, sj to the joining picot
       between the two chains that are before
       and after rings B and C on row 2

CH.   2, (mp, 2) x 4, sj to the small space at the
       base of ring D

CH.   2 (mp, 2) x 4, sj to the side of the drop
       bead

MR.   6, LP, 6, sj to the other side of the same
       drop bead

CH.   2, (mp, 2) x 4, sj to the small space at the
       base of ring E**

Repeat from * to ** five more times then cut
and tie to the start of the row and secure the
ends. Block and stiffen as required.

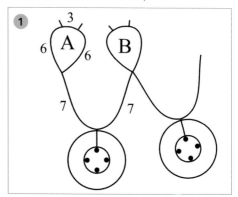

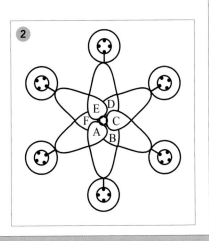

2

E D
F C
A B

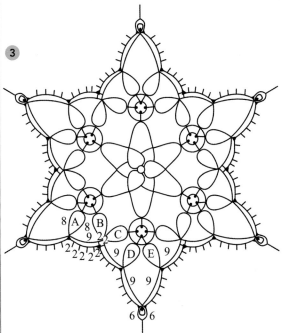

3

8 A
8 B
9
2 2 2 2 2
C
9
D E
9 9
9 9
6 6

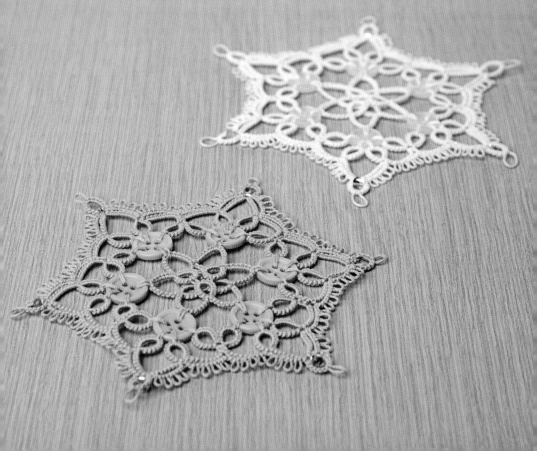

Hannah

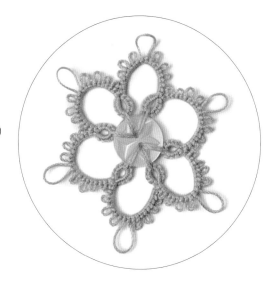

Materials:

Size 10 thread

1 x 15mm (⁵/₈in) two-hole button

Tools:

1 x shuttle

3 x picot gauges (an opened out paper clip for
   'p', cocktail stick for 'mp' and pencil for 'vbp')

1 x crochet hook, size 0.75mm (US 13)

Tapestry needle or beading needle

Small pair of scissors

Instructions:

Wind 1.5m (1¾yd) of thread onto the shuttle.
Do not cut.

R.A   5, + to one of the holes in the button,
       5, cl, RW

CH.   2, p, 2, p, 2, mp, 2, mp, 2, vbp, 2, mp,
       2, mp, 2, p, 2, p, 2, tension to measure
       about 2.5cm (1in), RW

R.B   5, + the same hole in the button, 5, cl,
       RW

CH.   As above

R.C   5, + the same hole in the button, 5, cl,
       RW

CH.   As above

R.D   5, + the other hole in the button, 5, cl,
       RW

CH.   As above

R.E   5, + the same hole in the button, 5, cl,
       RW

CH.   As above

R.F   5, + the same hole in the button, 5, cl,
       RW

CH.   As above

Cut and tie to the base of ring A, then secure
the ends. Block and stiffen as required.

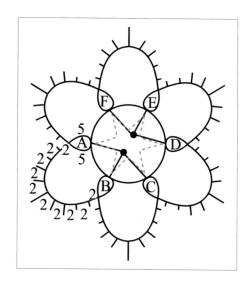

Ruth

Materials:
Size 20 thread

Tools:
2 x shuttles

1 x crochet hook, size 0.75mm (US 13)

Tapestry needle or beading needle

Small pair of scissors

Instructions:

Wind 2 shuttles CTM with about 3m (3¼yd) of thread onto shuttle 1 and 5m (5½yd) of thread onto shuttle 2.

SH.1   R.A   (See diagram 1) 8, p, 4, p, 2, p, 2, cl,

      R.B   2, + to ring A, 4, p, 6, cl, RW

      CH.   12, p, 2, SS, DNRW

SH.2   R.C   2, + to previous chain, 6, mp, 6, p, 2, cl

      R.D   2, + to ring C, 6, mp, 6, p, 2, cl, SS, DNRW

SH.1   CH.   2, + to ring D, 12, RW

      R.E   8, + to ring A, 4, p, 2, p, 2, cl

      R.F   2, + to ring E, 4, p, 6, cl, RW

      CH.   12, p, 2, SS, DNRW

SH.2   R.G   2, + to previous chain, 6, mp, 6, p, 2, cl

      R.H   2, + to ring G, 6, mp, 6, p, 2, cl, SS, DNRW

SH.1   CH.   (See diagram 2) 2, + to ring H, 12, RW

      R.I   8, + to ring E, 4, p, 2, p, 2, cl

      R.J   2, + to ring I, 4, p, 6, cl, RW

      CH.   12, p, 2, SS, DNRW

SH.2   R.K   2, + to previous chain, 6, mp, 6, p, 2, cl

      R.L   2, + to ring K, 6, mp, 6, p, 2, cl, SS, DNRW

SH.1   CH.   2, + to ring L, 12, RW

      R.M   8, + to ring I, 4, p, 2, p, 2, cl

      R.N   2, + to ring M, 4, p, 6, cl, RW

      CH.   12, p, 2, SS, DNRW

SH.2   R.O   2, + to previous chain, 6, mp, 6, p, 2, cl

      R.P   2, + to ring O, 6, mp, 6, p, 2, cl, SS, DNRW

SH.1   CH.   2, + to ring P, 12, RW

      R.Q   8, + to ring M, 4, p, 2, p, 2, cl

      R.R   2, + to ring Q, 4, p, 6, cl, RW

      CH.   12, p, 2, SS, DNRW

SH.2   R.S   2, + to previous chain, 6, mp, 6, p, 2, cl

      R.T   2, + to ring S, 6, mp, 6, p, 2, cl, SS, DNRW

SH.1   CH.   2, + to ring T, 12, RW

      R.U   8, + to ring Q, 4, + to ring A, 2, p, 2, cl

      R.V   2, + to ring U, 4, p, 6, cl, RW

      CH.   12, p, 2, SS, DNRW

SH.2   R.W   2, + to previous chain, 6, mp, 6, p, 2, cl

      R.X   2, + to ring W, 6, mp, 6, p, 2, cl, SS, DNRW

SH.1   CH.   2, + to ring X, 12, RW

Cut and tie to the base of rings A and B, then secure the ends.

Block to shape the chains as in the photo, and stiffen as required.

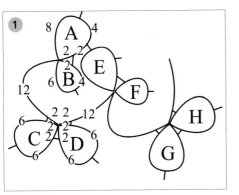

1
8 A 4
2 2
2
B 4
6
12 E
F
2 2
6 2 2 12
6 C 2 2 D H
6 2 2
6 6 G

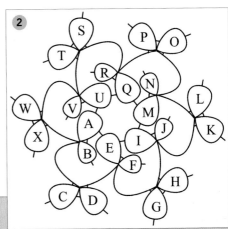

2
S P O
T R N
Q
W U L
V M
X A J K
B E I
F H
C D G

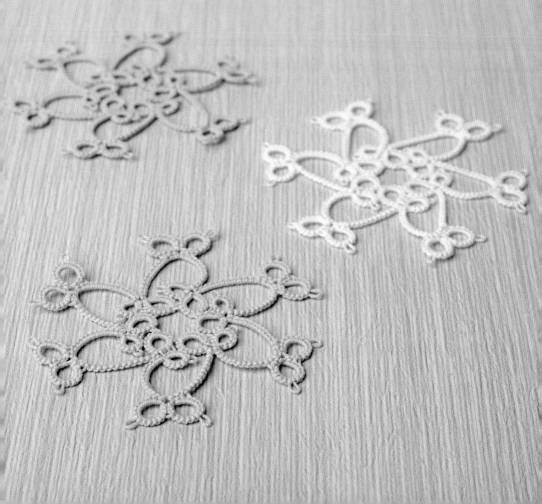

Gwyneth

Materials:

Size 20 thread

6 x size 4mm ($^3/_{16}$in) pearl beads

2 x jewellery finding split rings

2 x ear wires

1 x necklace bail

1 x chain necklace with clasp

Tools:

1 x shuttle

1 x fine needle

1 x crochet hook, size 0.75mm (US 13)

Small pair of scissors

Instructions:

Earrings (make 2)

Wind about 1m (1yd) of thread onto the shuttle. Do not cut.

R.A	3, p, 5, + to one of the jewellery finding split rings, 1, + to split ring again, 5, p, 3, cl, RW
CH.	2, RW
*R.B	3, + to previous ring, 5, mp, 5, p, 3, cl, RW (see diagram 1)
CH.	2, RW**

Repeat from * to ** three more times, then continue:

R.F	3, + to previous ring, 5, mp, 5, + to ring A (using the 'folded join' technique), 3, cl, RW
CH.	2

Cut, leaving ends about 15cm (6in) and tie to the base of ring A.

Using the fine needle, take both threads through the 4mm ($^3/_{16}$in) bead and tie them to the base of ring D. Secure the ends (see diagram 2).

Work the second earring, then block and stiffen the motifs as required. Attach an ear wire to each jewellery finding split ring.

Pendant

First snowflake motif

Wind about 1m (1yd) of thread onto the shuttle. Do not cut.

R.A	3, p, 5, + to the necklace bail (see diagram 3), 1, + to the necklace bail again, 5, p, 3, cl, RW
CH.	2, RW

Complete the first snowflake motif as for the earring snowflake motif.

Second snowflake motif

R.G	3, p, 5, + to ring E of 1st snowflake (see diagram 3), 5, p, 3, cl, RW
CH.	2, RW
R.H	3, + to ring G, 5, + to ring D of first snowflake, 5, p, 3, cl, RW
CH.	2, RW.

Complete the snowflake motif by following the instructions for rings C, D, E, F on the first motif.

Third snowflake motif

R.M	3, p, 5 + to ring I on 2nd motif, 5, p, 3, cl, RW
CH.	2, RW
R.N	3, + to ring M, 5, + to ring D on 1st snowflake, 5, p, 3, cl, RW
CH.	2, RW
R.O	3, + to ring N, 5, + to ring C on 1st snowflake, 5, p, 3, cl, RW
CH.	2, RW

Complete the snowflake motif as before (see diagram 3).

Fourth snowflake motif

R.S	3, p, 5, + to ring J on the 2nd snowflake, 5, p, 3, cl, RW
CH.	2, RW
R.T	3, + to ring S, 5, + to ring I on the 2nd snowflake, 5, p, 3, cl, RW
CH.	2, RW
R.U	3, + to ring T, 5, + to ring R on the 3rd snowflake, 5, p, 3, cl, RW
CH.	2, RW

Complete the snowflake motif as before (see diagram 3). Block and stiffen as required.

Anne

Materials:

Size 20 thread

1 x 2cm (¾in) diameter sequin

36 x size 11 beads

Tools:

2 x shuttles

1 x fine needle

2 x crochet hooks, size 0.75mm and
0.4mm (US 13 and 16)

Tapestry needle or beading needle

Small pair of scissors

Instructions:

Row 1

String 18 of the beads then wind about 2m
(2¼yd) of thread onto the shuttle, leaving
the beads on the ball thread. Do not cut (see
diagram 1).

R.A   4, p, 4, p, 4, cl, RW

CH.   5, B, 5, RW

*R.B   4, + to previous ring, 4, p, 4, cl, RW

CH.   5, B, 5, RW

Repeat from * three more times, then

R.F   4, + to previous ring, 4, + to ring A, 4, cl,
RW

CH.   5, B, 5 sj to the base of ring A, RW

Do not cut, continue on to row 2 h

Row 2 (see diagram 2)

R.G   4, p, 4, p, 4, cl, RW

CH.   4, B, 3, p, 3, B, 4, RW

*R.H   4, + to previous ring, 4, p, 4, cl, RW

CH.   4, B, 3, p, 3, B, 4, RW

Repeat from * three more times, then

R.L   4, + to previous ring, 4, + to ring G, 4, cl,
RW

CH.   4, B, 3, p, 3, B, 4

Cut and tie to the base of ring G, then secure
the ends.

Row 3 (see diagram 3)

String 18 beads then wind about 1.5m (1¾yd) of
thread onto the shuttle, leaving the beads on
the ball thread. Do not cut.

Fold row 1 on top of row 2, matching up the
rings. Use 3 beads for all beaded dpbs.

R.M   4, + through the base of one of the
rings on row 1 and to the base of the
corresponding ring on row 2 together, 4,
cl, RW

CH.   8, sj to the picot on the adjacent chain
on row 2

MR.N   8, beaded dpb, 8, tension then sj to the
same picot,

CH.   8, RW

*R.O   4, + to the base of the adjacent rings on
rows 1 and 2, 4, cl, RW

CH.   8, sj to the picot on the adjacent chain
on row 2

MR.P   8, beaded dpb, 8, tension then sj to the
same picot

CH.   8, RW

Repeat from * twice more, slip the large sequin
between rows 1 and 2 then work two more
repeats to complete the row. Cut and tie then
secure the ends. Block and stiffen as required.

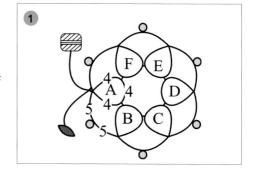

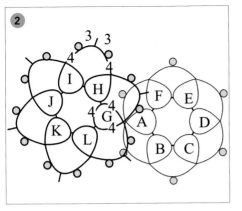

2

3 / 3
4
4
I
J   H
4
K 4 G 4
L A
F   E
D
B   C

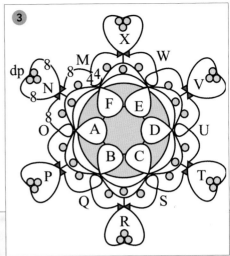

3

X
M   W
dp 8   8
N 4 4
8   F   E   V
O   A   D
B   C   U
P   T
Q   S
R

Sarah

Materials:
Size 10 or 20 thread

12 x 3.4mm (¹/₈in) drop beads

Tools:
1 x shuttle

1 x fine needle

2 x crochet hooks, size 0.75mm and 0.4mm (US 13 and 16)

Tapestry needle or beading needle

Small pair of scissors

Instructions:
Use 1 bead for all beaded dpb and beaded dpfs.

Row 1 (see diagram 1)

String 6 of the drop beads then wind about 2m (2¼yd) of thread onto the shuttle, leaving the beads on the ball thread. Do not cut.

R.A   5, p, 8, p, 8, p, 5, cl, RW

CH.   Work a beaded dpb, tension to 'encourage' into place, RW

*R.B   5, + to previous ring, 8, p, 8, p, 5, cl, RW

CH.   Work a beaded dpb, tension to 'encourage' into place, RW

Repeat from * three more times then

R.F   5, + to previous ring, 8, p, 8, + to ring A, 5, cl, RW

CH.   Work a beaded dpb, tension to 'encourage' into place

Cut and tie to the base of ring A then secure the ends.

Row 2 (see diagram 2)

String 6 drop beads then wind about 0.5m (½yd) of thread onto the shuttle, leaving the beads on the ball thread. Do not cut.

Join the thread to the picot between two of the rings on row 1.

*CH.   3, (p, 2) x 2, p, 1, beaded dpf, 1, (p, 2) x 2, p, 3, sj to the picot between the adjacent rings on row 1, tensioning the chain so that it sits just outside the ring.

Repeat from * five more times omitting the final sj. Cut and tie to the start of the row.

Row 3 (see diagrams 3 and 4)

Wind approximately 0.75m (¾yd) of thread onto the shuttle. Do not cut.

Join to the free picot on one of the rings on row 1.

Fold the chains to the front as you work this row.

*CH.   3, (p, 2) x 3, p, 1, vbp, 1, (p, 2) x 3, p, 3, tension to curve as in the picture then sj to the free picot on the adjacent ring on row 1.

Repeat from * five more times omitting the final sj. Cut and tie to the start of the row.

The chains of row 2 can be pulled forward a bit to give the snowflake a slightly 3D effect.

Block and stiffen as required.

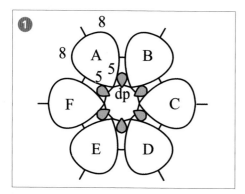

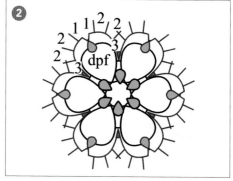

44

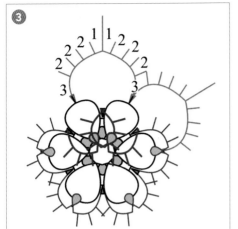

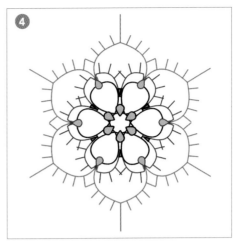

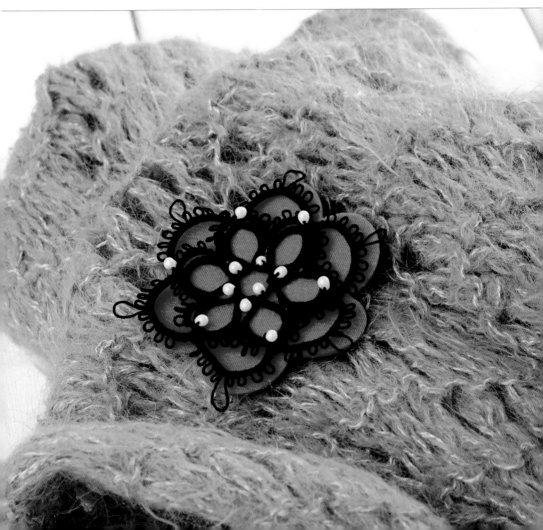

Christine

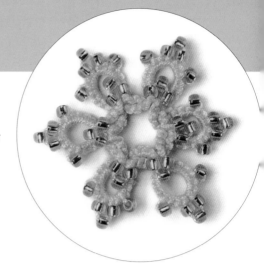

Materials:

Size 20 thread

48 x size 11 beads for each snowflake

Tools:

1 x shuttle

1 x Big Eyed Needle or beading needle

2 x crochet hooks, size 0.75mm and 0.4mm (US 13 and 16)

Small pair of scissors

Instructions:

Row 1

String 24 beads and wind about 0.75m (¾yd) of thread with 15 of the beads onto the shuttle, leaving 9 of the beads on the ball thread. Do not cut. Use 3 beads for all beaded dpbs.

R.A   (See diagram 1) Bring 5 beads from the shuttle into the ring round your hand, 5, B, 3, 3B, 3, B, 5, cl, RW

CH.   3, beaded dpb, 3, tension so that the dpb really curves down below the chain, RW

R.B   Bring 5 beads from the shuttle into the ring round your hand, 5, B, 3, 3B, 3, B, 5, cl, RW

CH.   3, beaded dpb, 3, tension so that the dpb really curves down below the chain, RW

R.C   Bring 5 beads from the shuttle into the ring round your hand, 5, B, 3, 3B, 3, B, 5, cl, RW

CH.   3, beaded dpb, 3, tension so that the dpb really curves down below the chain

Cut and tie to the base of ring A then secure the ends.

Work row 2 the same as row 1.

To assemble the snowflake, position row 2 on top of row 1 so that the six beaded rings are evenly spaced, then draw the beaded dropped picots of row 1 up through the centre of the snowflake so that they sit on top of the rings on row 2 (see diagram 2).

It is easier to do this if you block the snowflake by pinning the beaded dropped picots in place, then evenly space the rings before pinning them into position.

Block and stiffen as required.

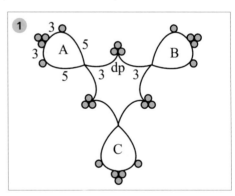

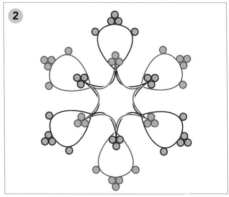

Acknowledgements
My special thanks to Hannah Crowle for
proof tatting my designs and to May Corfield
and the team at Search Press for enabling me
to produce this book.

Publishers' Note
For more designs and help with tatting techniques,
visit the author's website at
www.cariad-tatting.co.uk